Router
Canes

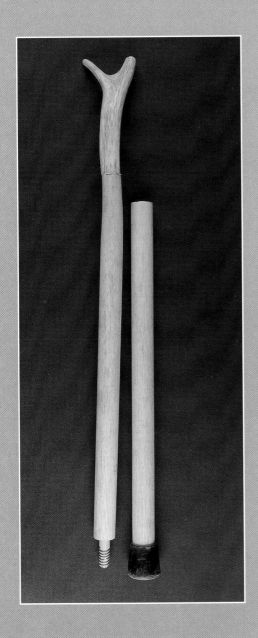

Dale Power

Text written with
and photography
by Jeffrey B. Snyder

Schiffer Publishing Ltd®

4880 Lower Valley Road, Atglen, PA 19310 USA

Contents

Introduction 3
   Patterns 4
Creating Router Canes 9
   "Rounding the Square Peg"—Using the Router to Turn
     Boards into Cane Shafts 9
   An Additional Way to Round Your Cane Shaft: A Dowel Turning Jig—
     for use on the router table 15
   Turning Handles 17
   Connecting the Two Halves of Your Traveling Cane's Shaft 22
   Creating an Eagle's Head Cane Handle 40
   Mounting the Eagle's Head Cane Handle 44
   Creating Rustic Canes with a Shaving Horse 45
   Fittings to Strengthen the Cane 51
   Decorating the Shaft 53
   Additional Handle Mounting Options and Additional Handles 57
   Finishing 60
Gallery 63

Copyright © 2002 by Dale L. Power
Library of Congress Control Number: 2001099105

Designed by John P. Cheek
Cover design by Bruce M. Waters
Type set in Americana XBd BT/Lydian BT

ISBN: 0-7643-1523-4
Printed in China

Published by Schiffer Publishing Ltd.
4880 Lower Valley Road
Atglen, PA 19310
Phone: (610) 593-1777; Fax: (610) 593-2002
E-mail: Schifferbk@aol.com
Please visit our web site catalog at
www.schifferbooks.com
We are always looking for people to write books on new and related subjects. If you have an idea for a book please contact us at the above address.

This book may be purchased from the publisher.
Include $3.95 for shipping.
Please try your bookstore first.
You may write for a free catalog.

In Europe, Schiffer books are distributed by
Bushwood Books
6 Marksbury Ave.
Kew Gardens
Surrey TW9 4JF England
Phone: 44 (0)20-8392-8585
Fax: 44 (0)20-8392-9876
E-mail: Bushwd@aol.com
Free postage in the UK. Europe: air mail at cost

Introduction

The Sphinx on antiquity offers up this riddle, "What starts on four legs, goes to two, and ends on three?" The answer is "Man." I will show you how to make that "third leg," the ever useful cane, in this book.

In this book, we will work our way step by step through the production of canes and walking sticks using the router and other tools that you have in your work shop. The difference between a cane (or walking stick), a staff, and a traveling or take-down cane will be illustrated in this book. As a good general rule of thumb, canes are roughly waist high, staffs are shoulder high, and traveling canes come apart in the middle of the shaft for easier transport when on the road.

By using the router and the largest straight cutting bit your router can handle, you can make canes from square stock without using a full-sized and expensive lathe. I will show you how to use different types of wood to make beautiful canes and walking sticks for yourself and others.

Tools Required

Here are the tools you will need to successfully complete these projects.
Router
Straight cutters
Hand saw
Wood lathe
Band saw
Table saw
Hack saw
Assorted hardware: t-nuts; carriage bolts; glue and a hammer.
If you are planning to do any carving, a good sharp knife is required.
Any soldering needed can be handled with a small propane torch.
Rubber gloves are needed to protect your hands when you are applying the stain.

Good luck with your work and have fun completing the projects in this book.

Dale Power

Patterns

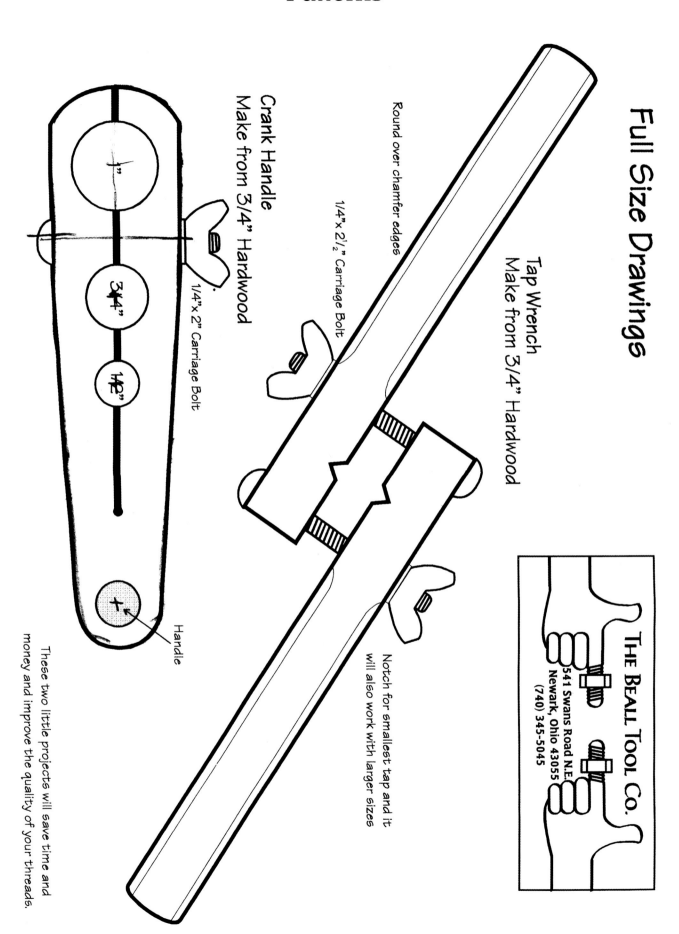

Full Size Drawings

Tap Wrench
Make from 3/4" Hardwood

Round over chamfer edges

1/4"x 2½" Carriage Bolt

Notch for smallest tap and it
will also work with larger sizes

Crank Handle
Make from 3/4" Hardwood

1/4"x 2" Carriage Bolt

1"

3/4"

1/2"

Handle

½"

These two little projects will save time and
money and improve the quality of your threads.

THE BEALL TOOL CO.
541 Swans Road N.E.
Newark, Ohio 43055
(740) 345-5045

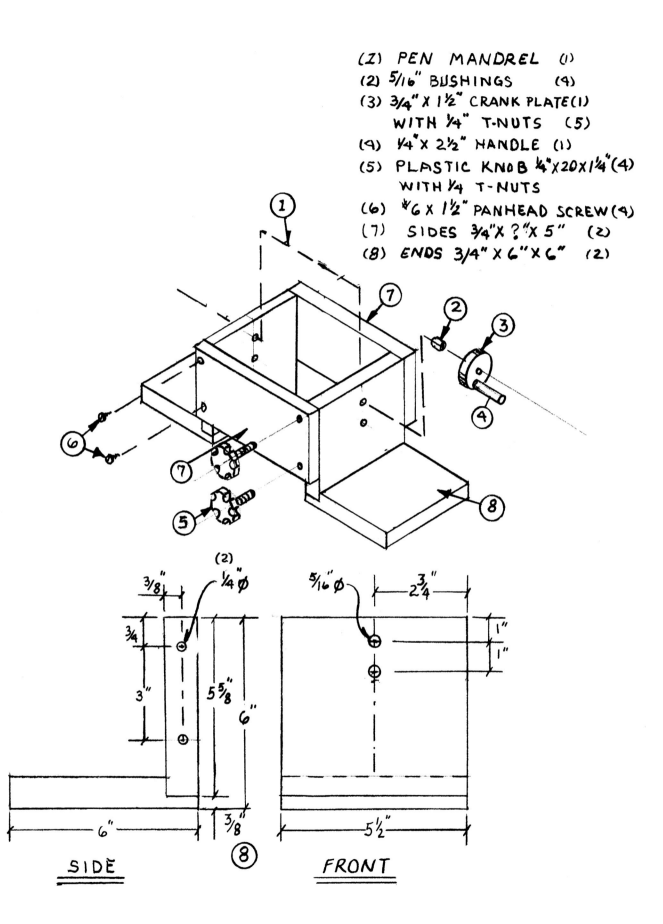

(1) PEN MANDREL (1)
(2) 5/16" BUSHINGS (4)
(3) 3/4" X 1½" CRANK PLATE (1)
    WITH ¼" T-NUTS (5)
(4) ¼" X 2½" HANDLE (1)
(5) PLASTIC KNOB ¼"x20x1¼" (4)
    WITH ¼ T-NUTS
(6) #6 X 1½" PANHEAD SCREW (4)
(7) SIDES 3/4" X ?" X 5" (2)
(8) ENDS 3/4" X 6" X 6" (2)

SIDE

FRONT

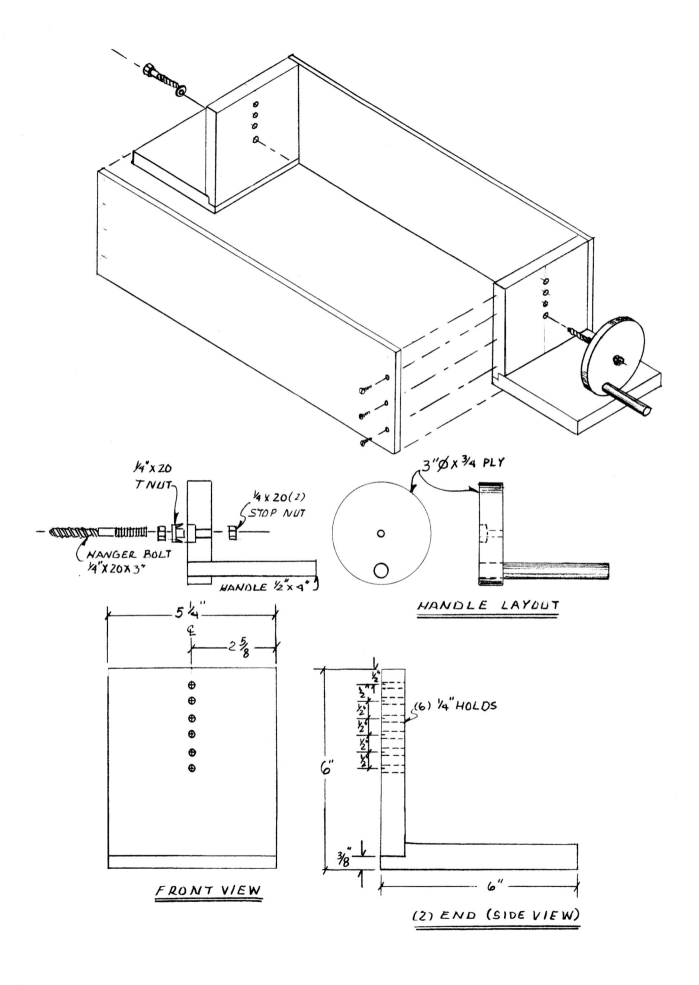

¼"x 20
T NUT

¼ x 20(2)
STOP NUT

HANGER BOLT
¼"x 20 x 3"

HANDLE ½"x 4"

3"Ø x ¾ PLY

HANDLE LAYOUT

5 ¼"

2 ⅝"

FRONT VIEW

(6) ¼" HOLDS

6"

½"
½"
½"
½"
½"
½"

6"

3/8"

(2) END (SIDE VIEW)

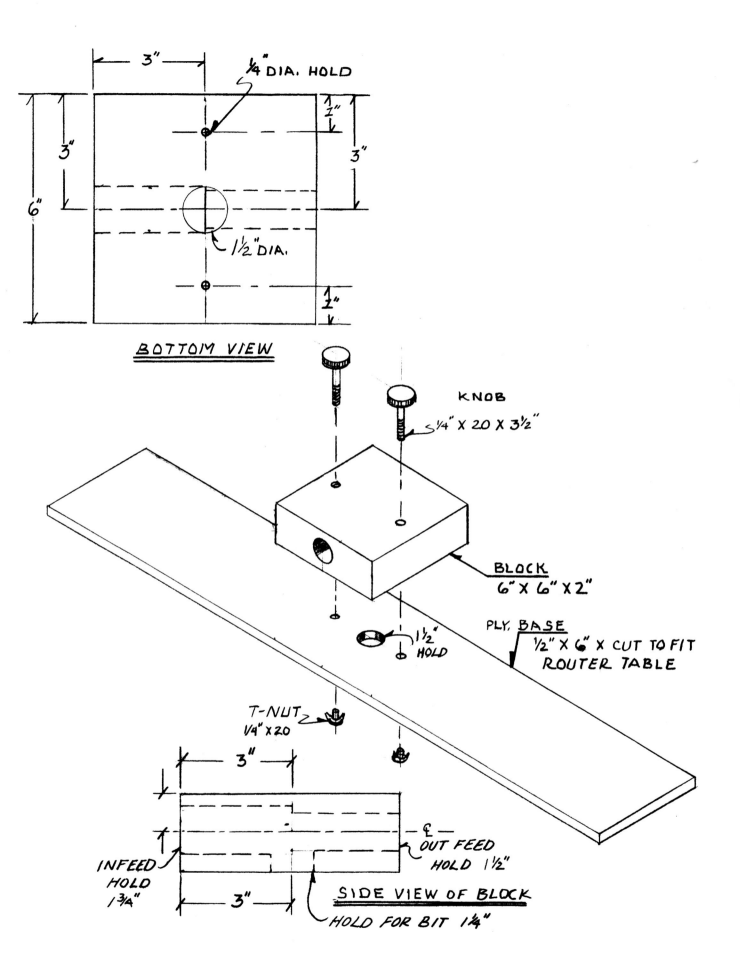

3"

¼" DIA. HOLD

½"

3"

3"

6"

1½" DIA.

1"

BOTTOM VIEW

KNOB

¼" X 20 X 3½"

BLOCK
6" X 6" X 2"

PLY. BASE
½" X 6" X CUT TO FIT
ROUTER TABLE

1½"
HOLD

T-NUT
¼" X 20

3"

INFEED
HOLD
1¾"

OUT FEED
HOLD 1½"

3"

SIDE VIEW OF BLOCK

HOLD FOR BIT 1¼"

7

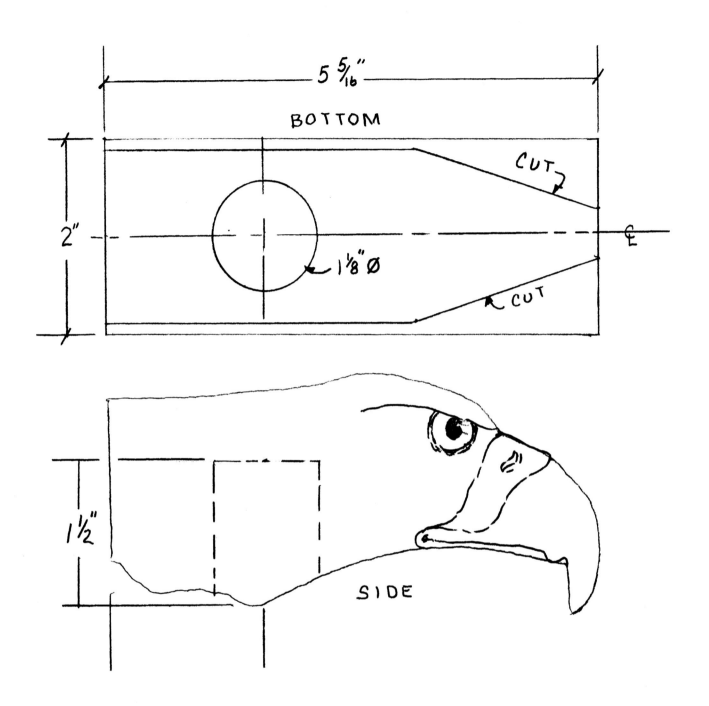

5 5/16"

BOTTOM

2"

CUT

CUT

℄

1 1/8" Ø

1 1/2"

SIDE

8

Creating Router Canes

"Rounding the Square Peg"—Using the Router to Turn Boards into Cane Shafts

Whenever working with any power tools, make sure that you have read—and that you have a clear understanding of—all the instructions. Always wear safety glasses and hearing protection. Leave all guards in place for your own safety. The guards have been removed here only for photographic purposes!

Use the table saw to create the first jig. Using a piece of scrap wood, cut your board about 7" x 7". This board will be used as a jig to help find the center of any rectangular length of wood that we may choose to round into a long, cylindrical cane shaft.

To cut a V shape in the wood, first measure to find the center of your board. Then set the blade to 45 degrees. Lower the blade enough so that your V cut will extend half way through the thickness of your wood.

Use a backer block to push the wood through the angled blade.

Rotate the wood 180 degrees and repeat the cut to complete your V cut.

The completed V cut.

Clamp the jig to the band saw table. Make sure that it is lined up square to the blade.

Rotate the wood and make the second cut, perfectly locating the center. Repeat this process on both ends.

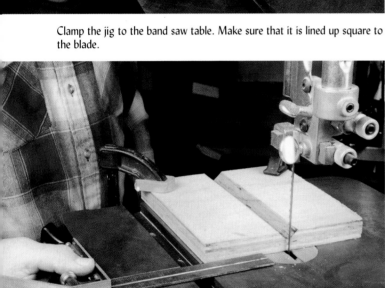

This jig will help your find the center of any rectangular piece of wood in the most efficient way prior to attempting to round the piece, no matter how you intend to round it. Line your rectangle of wood up in the guide in the jig and press it into the saw blade. This will give you an exact cut from corner to corner.

Notice that the center is located perfectly. This will work on a rectangle or square of any size.

Remember, any time you place wood into a lathe, no matter how well you believe it is centered, balanced, or fastened into the lathe, always stand off to the side when first starting it.

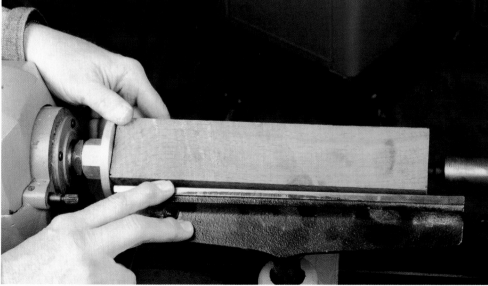

Make sure your tool rest is slightly higher that the half way point on the wood you are turning and square to the edge.

To check if your wood is round, lay the gouge over the top of the wood. If it bounces on the wood, it is not yet round.

Starting with a large gouge, knock off the corners to rough down your wood. This is not the length of wood you need to create a cane; however, this is a handy length for demonstration purposes to illustrate the steps necessary in rounding the cane shaft.

Continue rounding until you get to the proper size for the shaft.
A good project for turning practice is turning a handle for a walking staff.
We will work this demonstration piece down to make a walking staff.

An Additional Way to Round Your Cane Shaft:
A Dowel Turning Jig—for use on the router table

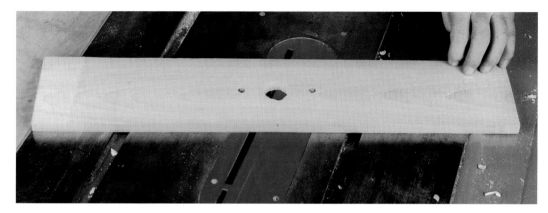

This is the base for a dowel turning jig. The base consists of a board measuring 6" x 24". The hole in the center is 1.5" in diameter to allow the router bit to come from the bottom up. Each of the holes on either side of the center hole is drilled to accommodate a 1/4 x 20 x 3 1/2" bolt. Brass inserts are fitted into the two side holes. If you do not have brass inserts, you can use T-nuts for the 1/4 x 20 x 3 1/2 bolts.

This block measures 6" x 6" x 2".

Then drill a 1 1/2" out-feed hole.

The hole on the bottom measures 1 3/4" in diameter.

The last two holes are drilled in the top of the block. These holes receive the 1/4 x 20 x 3 1/2" bolts. They correspond in location to the two in the holes in the base plate.

The jig is fully assembled and ready to set on the router table. The bit to be mounted to do the cutting is a 3/4" flat cutting bit. You can feed a 1 3/4" x 1 3/4" square board into the in-feed opening. By adjusting the router blade up or down and turning the board by hand, you will create a 1 1/2" round dowel that comes out of the out-feed hole. If after cutting the round dowel wobbles a bit in the hole, lower the bit slightly. If it won't go through, then raise the bit slightly.

If you prefer not to buy factory-made turn handles, you can make your own.

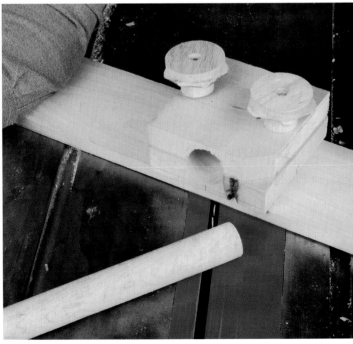

Here is a sample of the type of dowel you can turn out when your machine is set properly. With this device, you can use any of the special woods you may have around the house.

Turning Handles

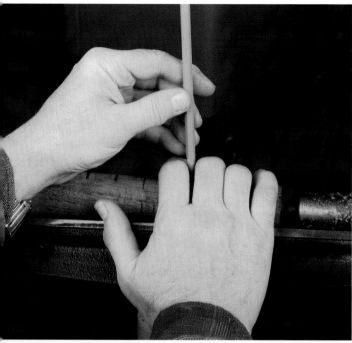

Left, center left, bottom left: We have enough wood here to turn two handles at once. Mark out for the finger grips on the two handles. Use a pencil to mark between your fingers. Once your marks are in place, turn on the lathe and apply the pencil to each mark to extend it around the handle shaft.

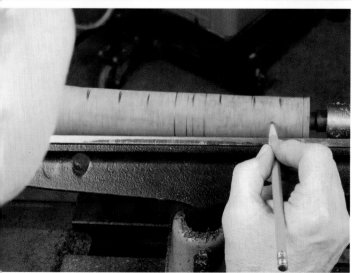

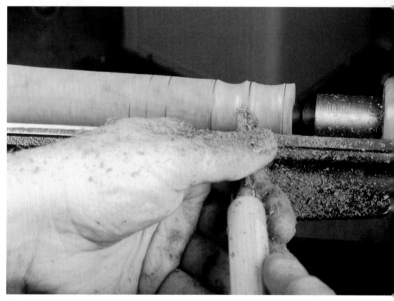

Using a small round gouge, clean out between the marks.

The finishing will be done with three grades of Scotch finishing pads. Apply each grade finishing pad, from the roughest to the finest, to the rotating handles in order to give them a smooth surface.

Round between the finger grooves to remove any hard edges.

Finish the top edge of the handle with any type of design that suits you. I'm using a small round gouge to put a decorative edge along the handle top.

The handle of your chisel makes an excellent burnishing tool.

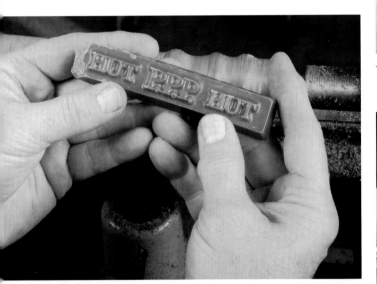

Finish the polish with the fine textured finishing pad. Apply enough pressure to ensure that the friction will create a little heat. This heat helps force the wax into the pores of the wood.

The finish for the handle is a permanent stick wax. Running the wax over the rotating handle applies an even, clean finish.

Continue polishing.

If you only want finger grooves on one side, use a rasp to remove the grooves from the opposite side.

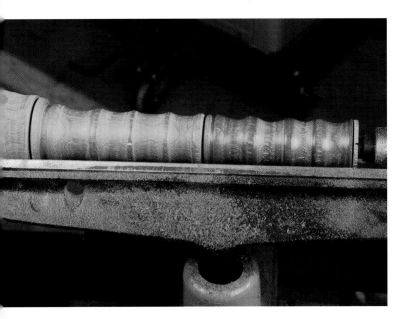

The second handle is turned out.

Once the grooves are removed, sand the handle again to smooth it down.

The finish on the second handle is Shellawax Cream, available from several sources, including Woodcraft Supply. This wax penetrates and seals raw wood well. It works equally well for handles of canes and walking sticks.

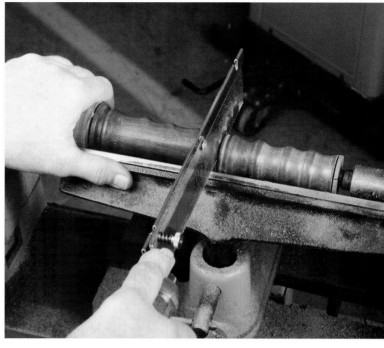

We are now ready to cut the two handle free from the mandrel using a back saw. If you rotate the handles as you go, you will get a better cut.

A final light buffing with the fine grade finishing pad makes the wax shine.

One handle is removed. Now remove the second handle from the mandrel.

Connecting the Two Halves of
Your Traveling Cane's Shaft

Adjust the height of the blade of the table saw so that the teeth are visible by 1/8" above the cane shaft to be cut.

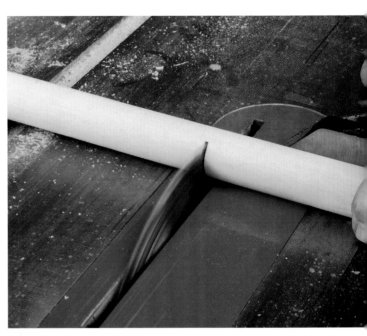

Cut two pieces of 1 3/8" doweling into two 18" lengths.

Don't trust the end of your dowel to be trimmed square. Trim it square yourself.

Clamp a block of wood on your table saw's blade to provide a measuring stop for your wood. This way, when the cutting is taking place there is no danger of binding. If you were to keep the blade against the dowel during cutting, the blade would likely bind on the wood, either damaging the wood or throwing the cut end of the dowel back in your face.

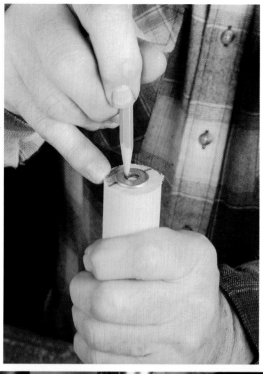

Finding the center of your dowel can be difficult. However, there are a few tricks to help out. One way to find the center is to take a washer of any size, placing it in the center of your dowel. This gives you a visual reference point when marking the center.

Drilling the center hole.

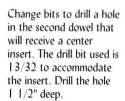

Change bits to drill a hole in the second dowel that will receive a center insert. The drill bit used is 13/32 to accommodate the insert. Drill the hole 1 1/2" deep.

I am using a homemade tool to install the brass insert. The handle consists of a 2 1/2" long 1/4 x 20 carriage pull. Insert that through a wooden ring. Place a nut on the bottom side to lock the carriage bolt to the handle. This makes it easier to install the insert into the wood at a square angle. The first thing you do is install the brass insert on the bolt in your homemade handle.

Use a 1/4" drill bit in a drill press to drill a hole in the dowel at the center mark. Use a tri-square to make sure your wood is straight vertically before you drill with the drill press. We are drilling holes to place an All Thread 1/4" x 20 that is 2 1/2" long.

Use a file to gently dress the metal that is sticking up along the edge.

Place your hand on top of the wooden circle. Apply downward pressure to the handle while turning it slowly clockwise to install the insert. This process will allow you to easily turn the metal insert into the appropriate hole and have it be square once inserted.

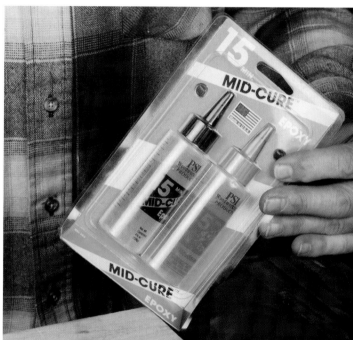

I suggest that you use 15 minute epoxy to hold the 1/4" threaded rod in place. To use the 15 minute epoxy, first mix equal parts of the two adhesives on a scrap you will throw away later.

Carefully clamp your threads so as not to crush the threading and cut off a 2 1/2" length with a hack saw.

Using a Popsicle stick, thoroughly mix your epoxy until the color is uniform.

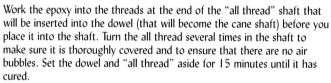

Work the epoxy into the threads at the end of the "all thread" shaft that will be inserted into the dowel (that will become the cane shaft) before you place it into the shaft. Turn the all thread several times in the shaft to make sure it is thoroughly covered and to ensure that there are no air bubbles. Set the dowel and "all thread" aside for 15 minutes until it has cured.

These steps are the basics for making any "take down" (or traveling) cane or walking stick. To size a walking stick for your own personal use, stand with your hand down to your side and make a fist. Measure from the center of your palm to the floor. Add 3/4" to this measurement and that should be the proper length for a cane. A walking stick, however, is usually 48" high at the point your hand meets the stick. A cane today is normally a medical device for supporting weight; a walking stick is used to maintain your balance on uneven ground.

Returning to the metal threaded insert: screw it into the other half of the cane shaft as previously shown if you have not already done so. This insert has the external threads necessary to screw it into the dowel's wood to hold it in place. No glue is required for this step.

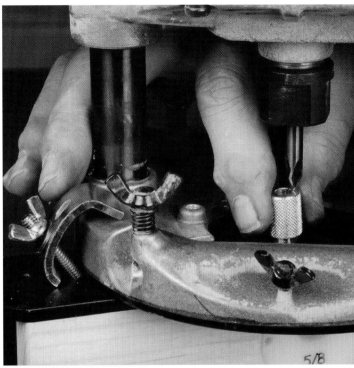

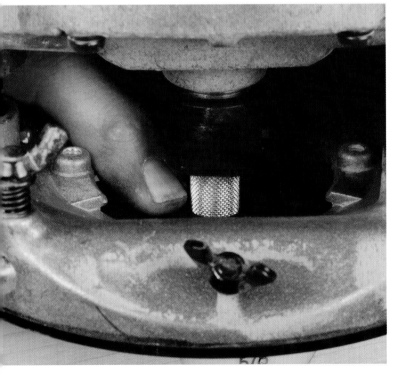

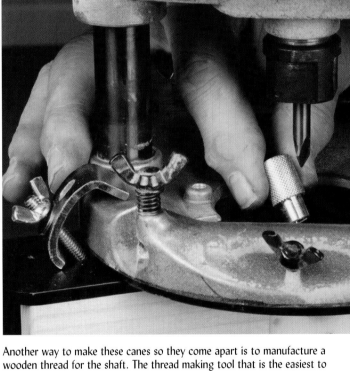

Another way to make these canes so they come apart is to manufacture a wooden thread for the shaft. The thread making tool that is the easiest to use is this Beall wood threader, made by the Beall Tool Company. A router is set in place above the platform. The router is centered by using a small aluminum insert that sits over the cutter blade. Once the router is centered, remember to remove the aluminum spacer.

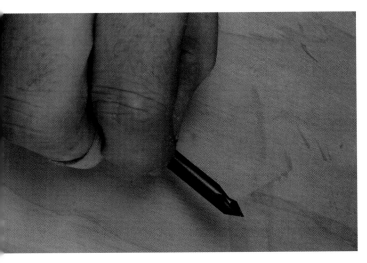

This is the bit required to cut the threads.

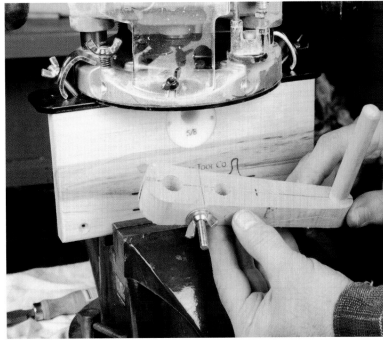

I suggest that you make a handle that will clamp onto your dowel as you move it into the device. This makes for a far more uniform thread as you run it in. Refer to the line drawings for the specifications for this handle.

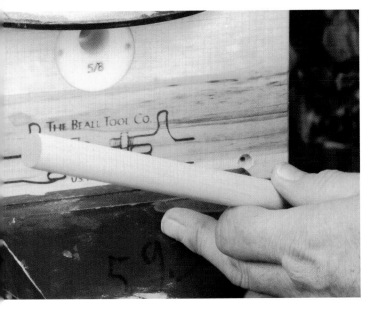

Use the best doweling you can find. Cheap doweling does not hold a uniform size. This is a good piece of 5/8" hardwood doweling.

Adjust the router so that the tip of the cutter is just visible inside of the tool opening.

A test cut may be necessary to find the correct depth for the threads. An simple way to determine if your threads are correct is to check whether the threaded doweling screws easily into the nylon area behind the cutter. It should. If the wooden threads do not screw in easily, lower the cutter a fraction of an inch and cut the threads again. If they are loose, raise the cutter a fraction and try again with another piece of doweling. Cut the treads.

Now it is time to manufacture the nut for the thread. To do that, take a good piece of hardwood, such as this black walnut, and drill several 1/2" holes spaced 1" to 1 1/2" apart. Cutting the holes with a 1/2" drill bit.

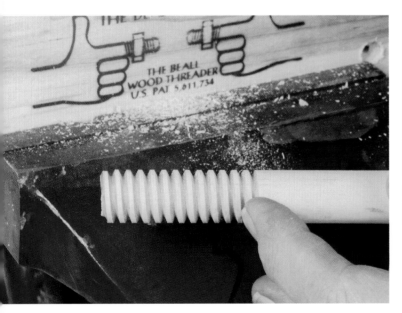

The threads are nicely cut.

Mount a tap on the drill press to cut the internal threads. This will assure that the holes are threaded square. This is the tap. Note that the first 1/2" end of the tap is smooth to help center it in the hole.

Turning the chuck by hand, cut the threads into the block of hardwood.

Once the holes are threaded into the hardwood, cut each piece loose with the band saw.

and glue it in place. Make sure the wooden nut is centered.

After thoroughly mixing the 15 minute epoxy, we apply it to the bottom side of the walnut nut . . .

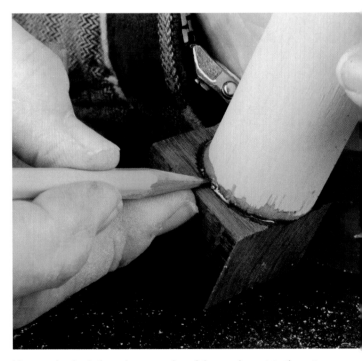

Measure the depth from the outer edge of the wooden nut to the outer edge of your cane staff and transfer that line to the outside edges of the nut so you have a guide line to follow when trimming away the excess wood with the band saw.

A Rounding Alternative

Cut off the excess wood, letting the saw do part of the scrap wood removal.

Attach the second half of the shaft to the nut. To see the nut rounded, go to page 39.

If you don't have a lathe to turn on, now is the time to make this jig. The jig will allow you to use your router to turn a cane shaft from some special stick you have been saving for this purpose. First, cut 3/4" plywood to make four pieces 5 1/2" x 5 1/2" on the table saw.

Now make a rabbit cut to join the two pieces of plywood together in a stronger joint. Mark the location at the depth the rabbit is to be cut.

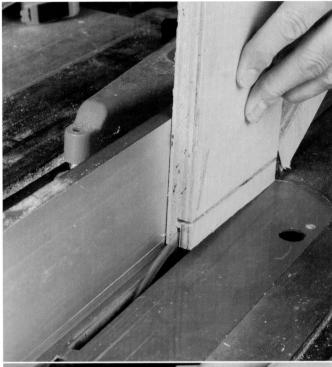

Adjust the height of the table saw blade to 1/2" and make your first cut.

To finish the rabbit, set the wood up on edge and reset the fence and the height of the blade to 3/4".

The rabbit cut is complete. The two pieces of 3/4" plywood will fit together like this.

Draw a center line. Mark the locations for a series of ˘" holes to be drilled along that center line. These holes begin 1" in from the edge, with a hole every 1/2" after that. Stop at 3 1/2".

Marking the measurements.

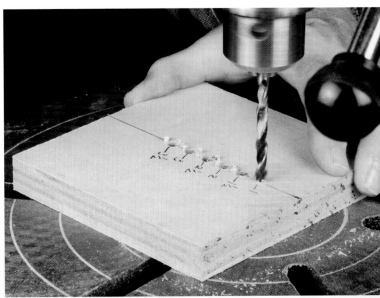

Drilling the 1/4" holes at the measured spots.

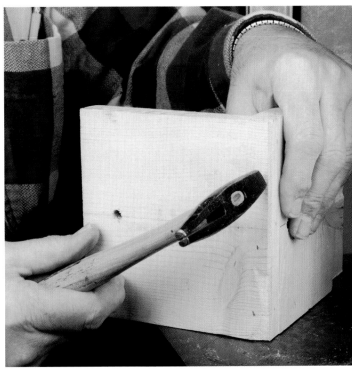

After gluing and nailing the ends together, we need to provide plywood sides to complete the jig. The plywood sides measure 4" x 2" in length.

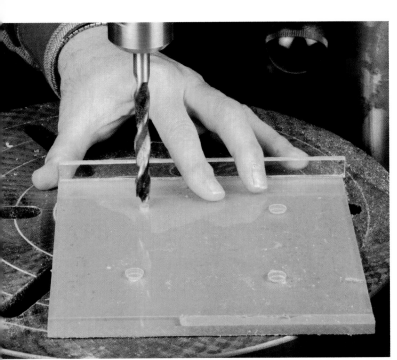

After drilling the 1/4" holes, counter sink holes into this router plate, to put the screws that hold the plate to the bottom of the router well below the plate's surface. We are using a 13/32" bit to make the counter sink holes.

Trim the router plate to fit the side supports of the jig.

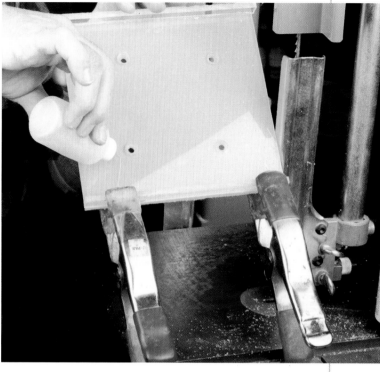

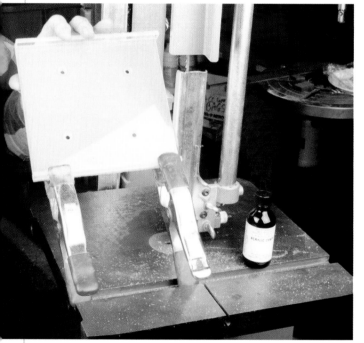

Take the piece just trimmed from the side of the plate, clamp it in place with a couple of spring clamps, and adhere it in place with acrylic cement. Use the applicator that comes with the glue to apply it. In this way you form the guides for the router.

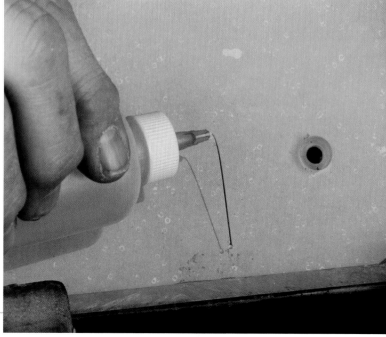

Cut a 2 1/2" circle, center drill it to receive a T-nut, and fit it with a wooden dowel for a turn handle.

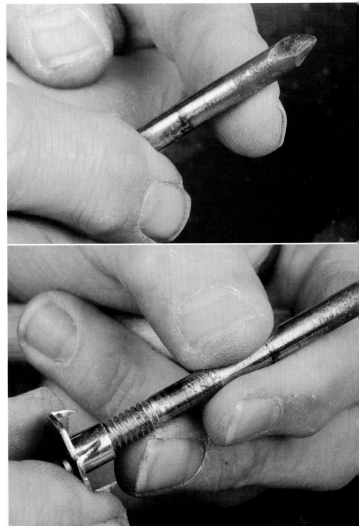

Attaching the sides of the support piece for the jig. This finishes out the bracket.

Cut the head off of a 3" carriage bolt. Grind or file the area where the head was to a point. Screw on a T-nut . . .

and place it through the handle.

Pre-mount a 3/4" square cutting router bit in the router.

After mounting the 1 1/2" x 1 1/2" square wooden piece in the jig, we will ready the router by making a template to fit over this jig.

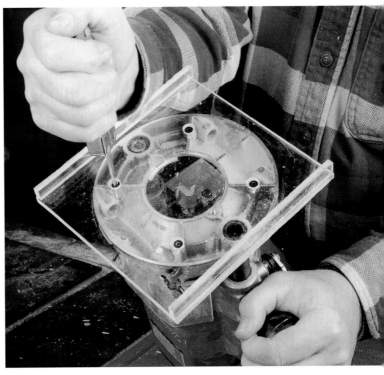

Lower the bit down so that it is below the surface of the router plate itself. Attach the bottom plate.

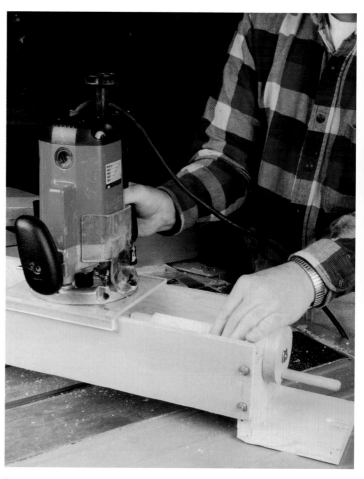

Set the router for about half the depth of the material you want to remove. While routing, rotate the handle with one hand while guiding the router with the other.

To simplify things, we will not have to find the center for the bit on the guide plate. We will let the bit cut its own hole. While cutting the hole, place the router and guide on top of a scrap block of wood to keep from fracturing the Plexiglas.

Continue to route, working your wood down until you achieve a round dowel. A little practice turning and moving the router and you can achieve a very smooth dowel like this. This dowel can be up to 2 1/2 feet long and any size from 1/2" to 3" if you desire. Note: if you want to make a tapered dowel, set one end down into the next hole. Do not reset the router; just continue to route and you will make a tapered dowel out of it.

Rounding the Nut

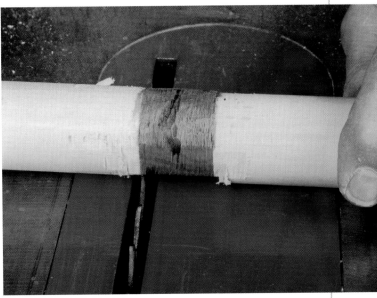

You may remove most of the waste material from the nut by placing the table saw blade down low enough that it just removes the excess from the nut. Then you can finish rounding with the rasp.

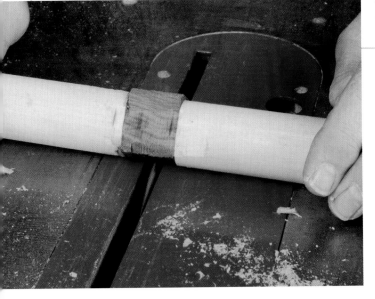

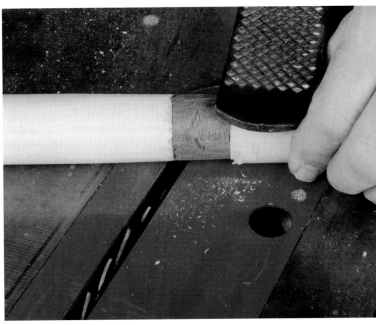

Dressing down the nut with the rasp. Now you can fine sand and finish the shaft with a clear finish or any stain you wish.

Creating an Eagle's Head Cane Handle

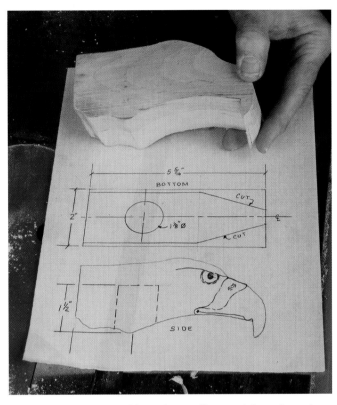

This eagle's head handle will be made out of basswood. It can be made from any wood with a high tensile strength, such as maple or black walnut, as well. Refer to the drawing for the measurements for the wood you will need. After transferring the drawing to the wood, rough out the block on the band saw.

Remove the excess wood from the beak area with the band saw.

Place a centerline on your piece in pencil.

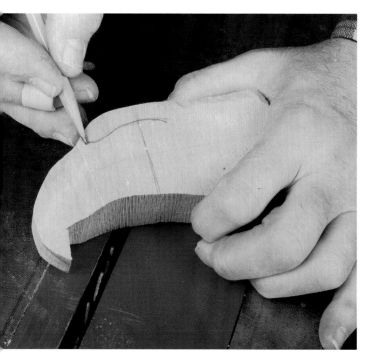

Now draw in areas you do not want to remove, like the eagle's brow.

Round off the edges so that you can hold the handle comfortably. Frequently grip the handle in your hand as you would hold a cane to make sure the handle is comfortable.

Rough out the shape of the cane head itself to see how much wood must be removed.

With a knife, place a stop cut along the eyebrow area.

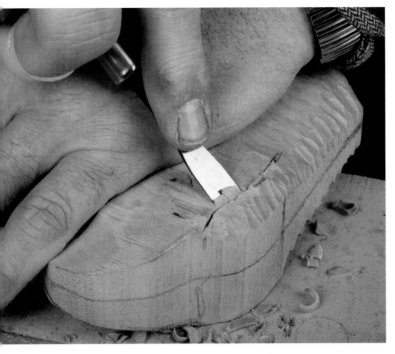

Relieve the excess wood to that stop cut with a flat gouge.

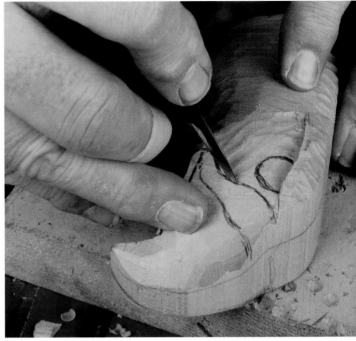

Use a fine bladed knife to place a stop cut along the beak and the head join and also around the eye.

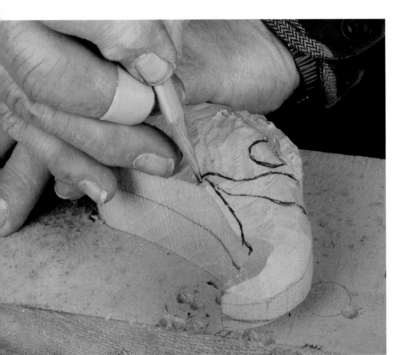

Sketch the beak and the eye in place prior to cutting them down.

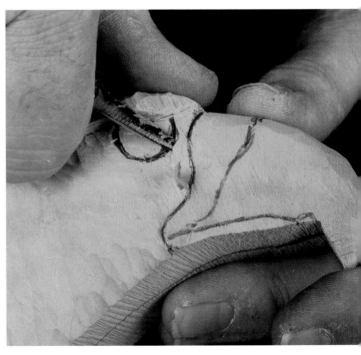

Remove the excess wood down to the stop cuts with the tip of the knife.

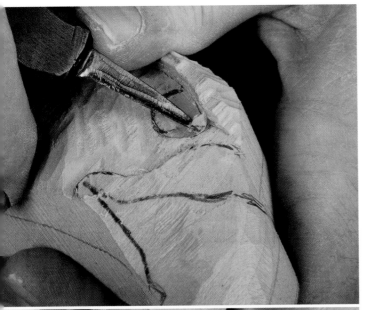

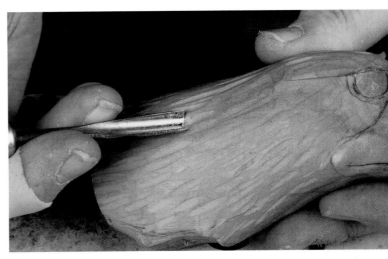

Continue rounding off the head until you reach a finished piece you are satisfied with, like this. After the rounding is finished, the feathers may be cut in with a small gouge.

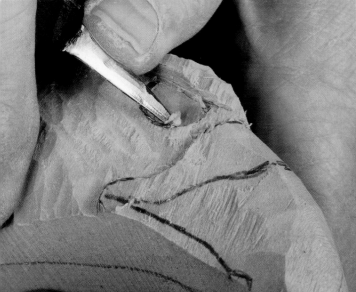

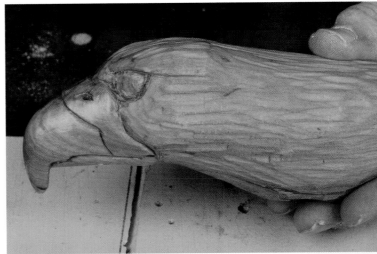

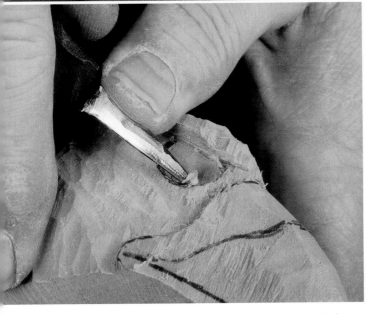

Form the eye by rounding down, removing excess wood from inside the eye down to the stop cut around the outer edge of the eye.

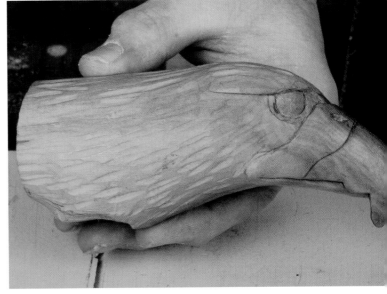

The finished carving.

Mounting the Eagle's Head Cane Handle

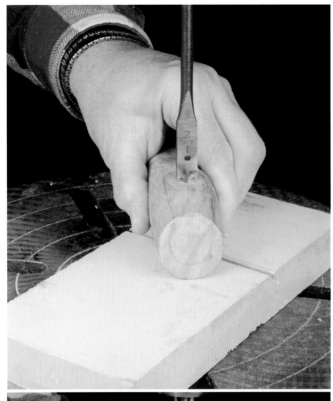

With the epoxy resin glue, we are attaching the head to the doweling and to the top of the cane. To ensure a proper fit between the cane top and handle, I would suggest you dry fit it first and make sure you have a good flat area for the cane to attach to. Make sure there are no sharp corners sticking out past the cane head. The head is now in place.

Now it is time to cut a hole in the handle base to accommodate a piece of 5/8" dowel rod using the drill press. This hole must measure over half way through the handle height, a total of 1 1/2" into the handle in the case of this eagle's head.

Creating Rustic Canes with a Shaving Horse

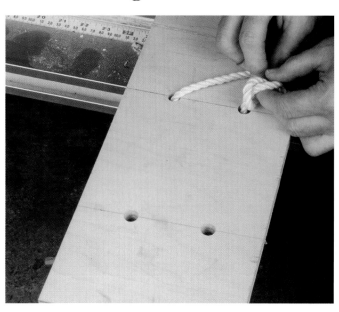

Start to assemble a rope vise by inserting rope through the rear right hole and down through the rear left hole. Tie the rope off on the rear right side.

Now it is time to make an alternative to a shaving horse. This is a type of clamp called a "foot operated clamp." It is quite popular in the Orient. First, using a piece of 3/4" plywood or equivalent board, over 24" long (although 30" long is better), drill two sets of holes, one set at 4" and another at 10" from the edge. Drill your holes at least 2" in from the sides.

All four holes are now in place.

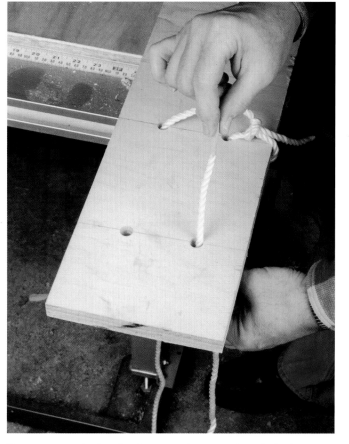

The rope crosses back under the piece and come up through the front right hole.

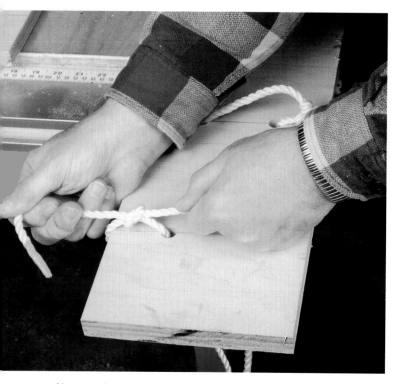

Now pass the rope down through the front left hole and tie it off, adjusting the length so the rope does not come all the way down to the floor.

Use a draw knife to remove the bark, if you so desire.

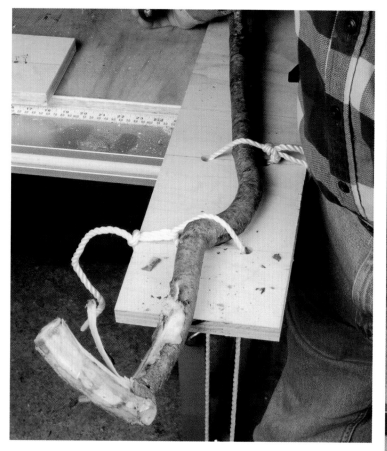

To illustrate how this works, first insert any one of the canes you may be working with through the loops above the board. Now, place your foot through the rope loop hanging down. This action will tighten the ropes over the cane, securing it to the board.

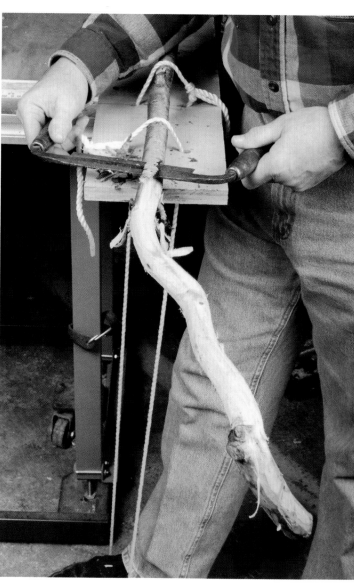

We are removing the bark from a cherry stick naturally shaped in the form of a cane.

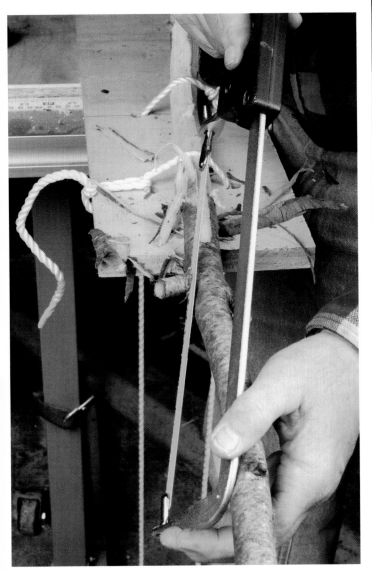

If there are some knots on the shaft you don't want, use a hack saw to remove them.

This is a half circle spoke shave. It works very well for taking off the under bark or sapwood of the cane.

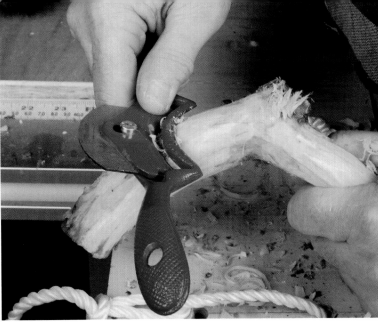

Finishing the removal of the under bark from the handle.

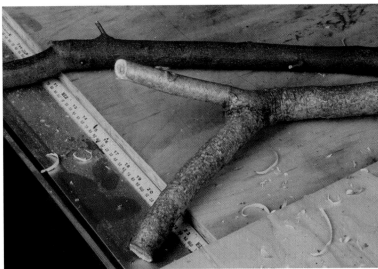

Taking advantage of the natural fork in this stick, we will make an unusually shaped cane.

First mark the two arms of the fork at the same length. We will remove excess wood beyond these marks so that the handle, when mounted across the limbs of the fork, will be level.

47

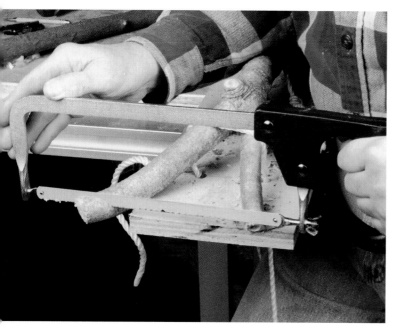

Use a hack saw to cut off the excess wood. In this case, excess wood needs to be removed from only one arm. The reason to use a hacksaw is that the hacksaw's finer teeth give you a finer cut.

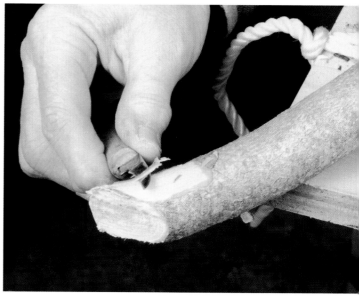

Removing the bark.

Determine how much of the bark to remove to insert the cross handle. Use the tri-square to mark the forks. Remove roughly 1" of bark from the ends of the fork.

The bark is removed.

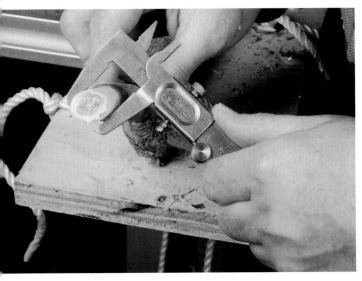

Now measure the smaller limb of the Y to drill a hole of the same diameter in the wooden cross piece that will be the handle. This measurement will be used to create a template to use during the reduction of the exposed wood of the thicker limb to make the two match in size. That way only a single drill bit will be required when drilling holes in the cross bar prior to fitting it to the Y.

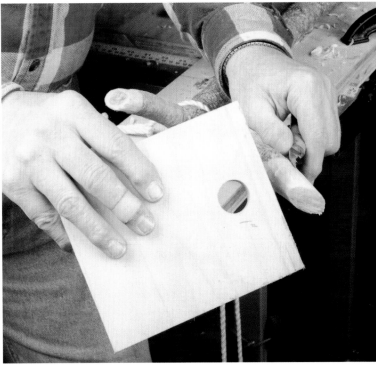

Use the template to reduce the diameter of the larger limb to match that of the smaller limb. Cutting down the larger fork of the Y.

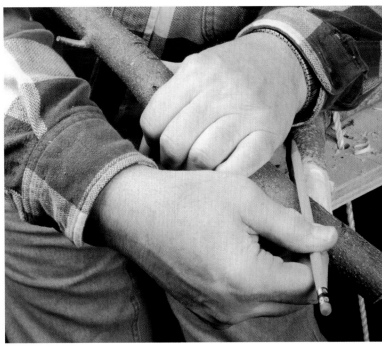

Determining the angle of the hole to be drilled for one shaft of the Y. Each shaft will need its own custom drilled hole as each has a different angle.

Drilling a 1" hole in a wood scrap for the template.

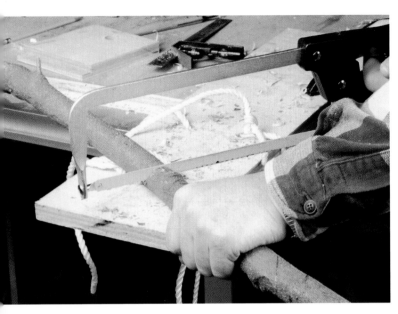

Cut the crosspiece handle to length with the hacksaw. Cutting it to length makes it easier to handle during drilling.

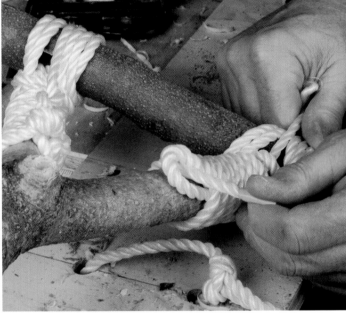

Once the holes are drilled, secure the crosspiece to the Y of the cane. To add interest to this plain cane, add rope lashings to the Y to create a nautical theme. Leave a loop of rope down the shaft and wrap rope around the shaft down to the end of the loop. Put the end of your rope through the loop and pull back up, securing your rope.

Secure the crosspiece handle at the proper angle to cut the hole you need for each branch of the Y.

The finished handle.

Fittings to Strengthen the Cane

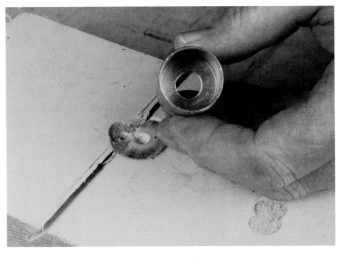

The washer is now in place in the middle of the fitting.

Here is a way to use an "off the shelf" item to support the joint where the two halves of your cane shaft are connected together. Using this brass pipe fitting with a washer soldered into the middle makes a very good support where the joint comes together. Use a propane or butane torch to do the soldering as a soldering iron does not get quite hot enough to work with this material.

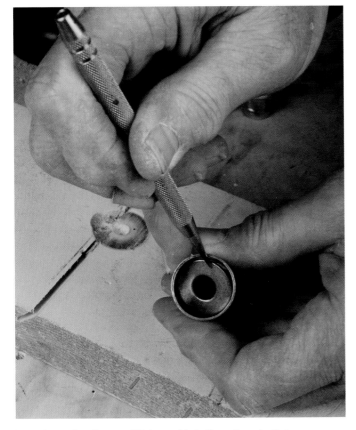

With the butane torch, heat the outside of the fitting. Place solder on the inside of the fitting along the edge where the fitting and washer touch, allowing the solder to run around the edge of the joint as it melts. Continue this process until you have a bead of solder completely around the outer edge of the washer.

Push the washer down until it is roughly half way into the fitting.

The washer is soldered in place.

Use a rasp to reduce the cane diameter. The cane shaft should slide easily into the brass fitting.

Test fit to make sure the diameter is correct.

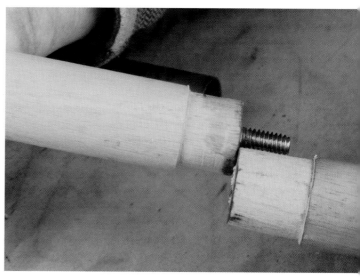

Work down both the top and bottom portions of the shaft.

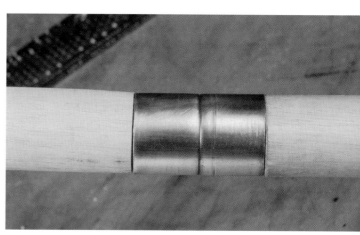

The two halves of the cane shaft should now fit easily together at this firm and well-supported joint.

For a finishing touch at the base of your cane, there are furniture leg brass decorations at the hardware store that work well on the base of a cane. Reduce the base of the shaft to fit the brass decorative tip.

Decorating the Shaft

Now, let's discuss creating a spiral decoration for the cane shaft. As a reminder, always square the end of your dowel before measuring. The dowel, as it comes from the store, is not always square.

The dowel has been cut. Make sure all your cuts are square.

Mark the dowel for cutting at 18".

To find the center of any dowel, no matter what size, first visually reference the center with a pencil mark. Next, hold your finger against the side of the dowel and swing an arc across the dowel with your pencil. Rotate the dowel and repeat this process, swinging arcs until you end up with a flower shape. The center of your flower will be the center of the dowel.

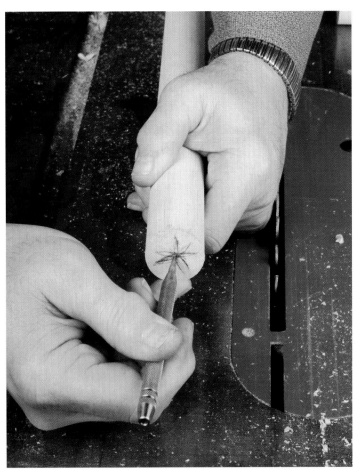

Take a piece of wood and clamp it to a push or pull saw, creating a depth stop for a uniform cut. The cut will be approximately 3/32" deep. The depth of the cut can be adjusted according to your personal preference.

Punch a hole at the center of the dowel with a small awl.

If you have the luxury of a lathe, attach the face plate to one end of the dowel.

To create a pattern for your spiral cut, first make a spiral pattern on the dowel using 3/4" masking tape.

Draw a pencil line roughly down the center of the tape. This will be the line you cut with the saw to make the center of the spiral.

Using a square nose chisel, remove the wood from the outer edge of the tape to the bottom of the saw cut. It does not matter where on the spiral you begin. Your cuts do not have to be perfect, as we are aiming for a rustic look to this spiraling decoration.

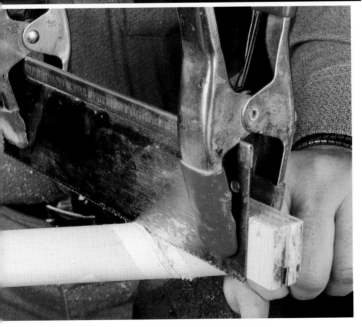

Take the saw and cut along your pencil lines as you turn the dowel. Continue to cut until the depth stop rests on the wood. You can use either a push or pull saw.

Continuing along the spiral. If you want the look of a wider spiral, cut the other side of the tape in the same manner. Here only one half has been cut for a narrower design.

The spiral completed.

Clean up the cuts left by the chisel with a rasp so the spiral will be more uniform. If you prefer the more rustic look of the chisel cuts, this step can be eliminated.

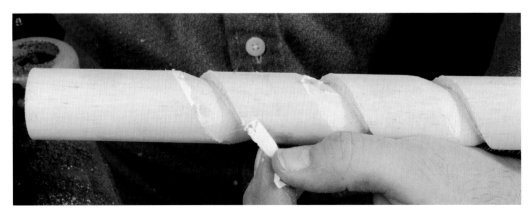

Remove the remaining masking tape. The rasp or a piece of sandpaper can be used to remove the small bits that don't come off easily by pulling.

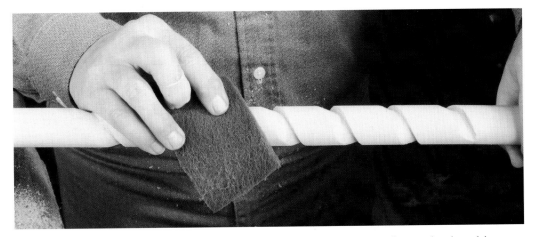

A small abrasive pad works well for removing any small slivers of wood that may have torn loose at the edges of the cuts.

The piece is ready to be removed from the lathe.

Additional Handle Mounting Options and Additional Handles

At this point, refer back to the instructions for setting both all thread and brass connectors into both halves of the cane shaft to finish your spiraling design traveling cane shaft halves.

For seal the all thread in place at the joint of your spiral cane, first mix equal parts of epoxy resin thoroughly until you have a uniform color.

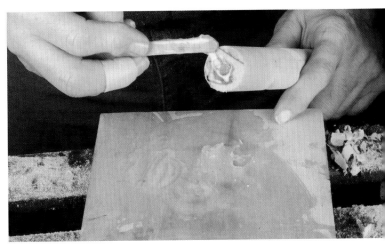

Place the resin in the hole on the end of the spiral dowel.

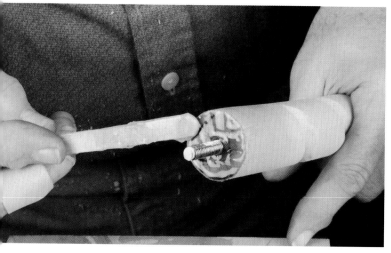

Excess resin can just be wiped across the end of the dowel to provide a harder surface for the joint to touch. Set aside to cure. We are now ready to attach the handle. First drill the handle center with a 13/32" drill bit. Place a brass threaded insert, as shown earlier, into the handle using the round driver. Attach the handle.

An alternate handle style can be made from a deer's antler. Here are some sample deer's antlers that could be used. The one being mounted has been trimmed on the ends using a hack saw (any other saw with a fine tooth pattern would also work). The bolt has been drilled and countersunk into the antler to keep it from turning while being screwed into place. If desired, the bolt hole could be filled with an epoxy mixture to simulate a decorative stone such as turquoise. Notice the copper fitting to help support the junction where the handle and the cane come together. Using an abrasive pad will shine up this fitting nicely, if so desired.

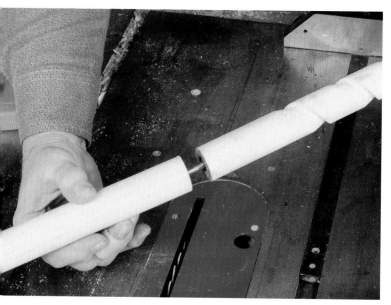

Before attaching the handle, join the upper half of the spiral cane shaft with the lower straight half (no spiral design) of the walking stick by screwing the all thread into the threaded brass insert, which has been added using the same steps shown previously.

To protect the end of the cane from wear and tear as it hits the road surface while you are walking, you can purchased nail on plastic gliders at a hardware store. Simply nail a glider in place on the bottom end of the cane. This spiral cane is now complete, except for the finishing.

Using the brass insert we have already set into the handle, connect the handle and spiral decorated upper half of the cane shaft.

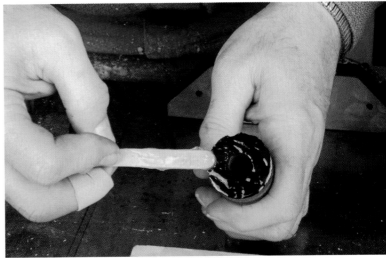

Now repeat this process on the handle. Spread the epoxy out along the outside rim of the handle so that you will have good contact between the cane and the handle.

If you want to mount a handle permanently on a cane, here is a way to do it. Drill a 5/8" hole in the handle and the top of the cane.

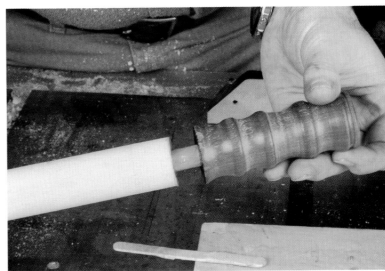

Apply epoxy on a 5/8" dowel and make sure there are no dry spots. Insert the dowel into the cane with half of the dowel exposed above the top edge of the cane and then push the handle down on the top of the remaining exposed doweling.

Now attach the handle with a 5/8" dowel and epoxy resin. First "stuff" the hole with enough epoxy resin to make sure you have good coverage all the way around your dowel.

Apply pressure to the handle to be sure you have a solid connection. This permanently attached handle works very well on walking sticks and other canes that are not designed to be weight bearing.

Finishing

On a rustic walking stick, use a small scraper to clean the wood, smoothing out any blemishes. Any areas that are not scraped down to a smooth white finish will turn very dark when you apply the finish. Keep this in mind if there are any areas you particularly want to highlight with the finish.

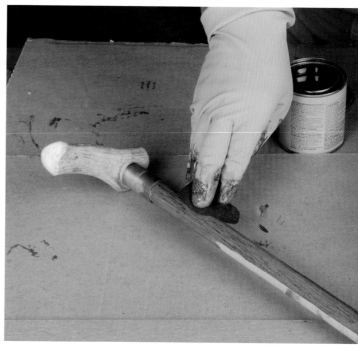

I am applying the same finish to the cane with the antler handle. This wood will take the stain differently than the green wood, so we will wipe it off after only five minutes.

We will be using a wipe on, rather than a paint on, finish. The directions on the can of wood stain note that for the best results, the wood should be clean, oil free, and dry. Liberally apply the stain. After the stain is applied, let it set for five to fifteen minutes, depending on how dark you want the finish to be. The excess is then wiped off. Gloves are recommended when using this stain. Oil finishes of this type do not dry quickly, so you should not have any lap marks where you have started or stopped the application. Set the stained cane aside to dry.

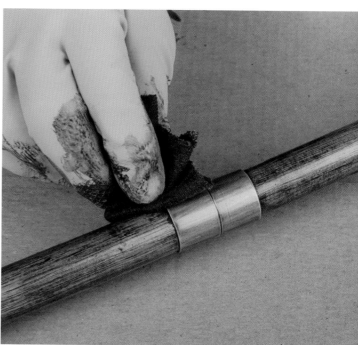

Don't worry about being too careful around the copper fittings Go right over them with the stain, as we will buff them up later.

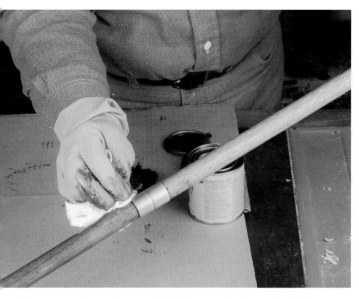

The excess stain on the upper half of the cane has been wiped off.

Wiping the stain off the rustic stick. The stain was left on this green wood for approximately ten minutes, so it has soaked in quite a bit.

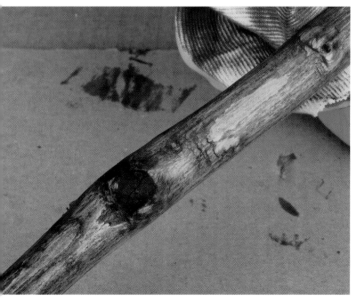

Knots and other rough areas will stain much darker.

Note the difference in darkness between the areas that were smoothed with the scraper and those that were left unscraped.

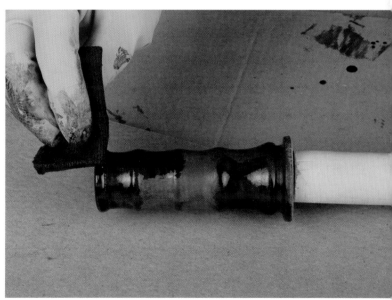

For the spiral walking stick, first use one of the coarser polishing pads to clean up any rough areas around the spiral. This clean up will help keep any chipping to a minimum and will also allow the stain to penetrate better. Even though the handle is black walnut, applying stain to it will accentuate the difference in the woods even more.

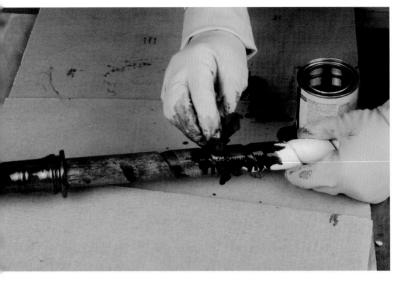

Flood the entire stick with the stain.

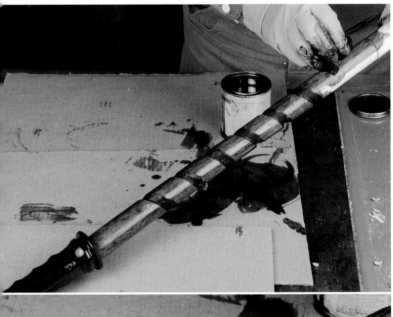

The cut areas will take the stain even more than the smooth surfaces. Be aware that any nicks or scratches on the surface will show. Smooth these blemishes out ahead of time if you don't want them to be revealed.

The staining of the spiral walking stick is completed. If you want to apply a clear coat of finish, you can do so after eight hours. Otherwise, let the cane dry for twenty-four hours.

Here is another cane head style, similar to a design used by women in the late nineteenth century.

Gallery

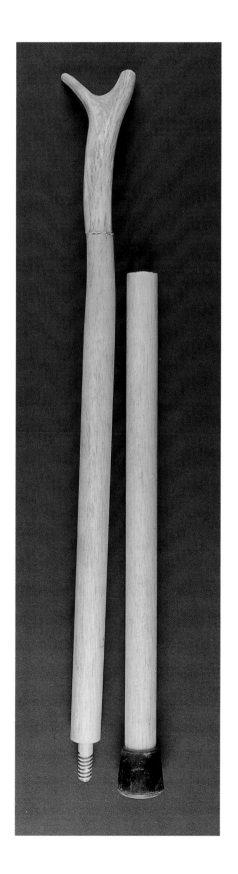

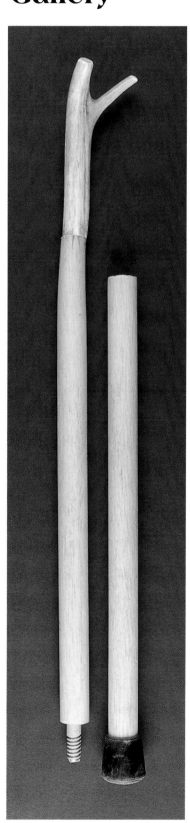

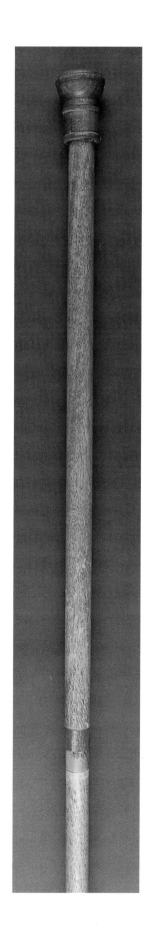

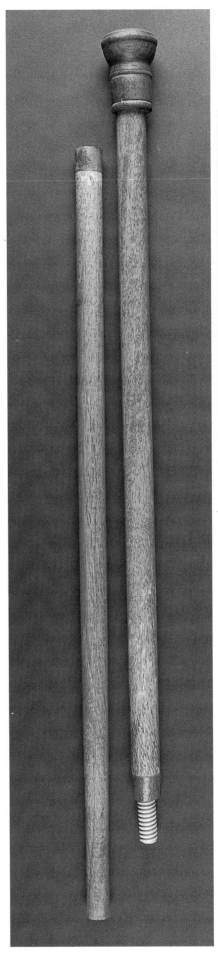

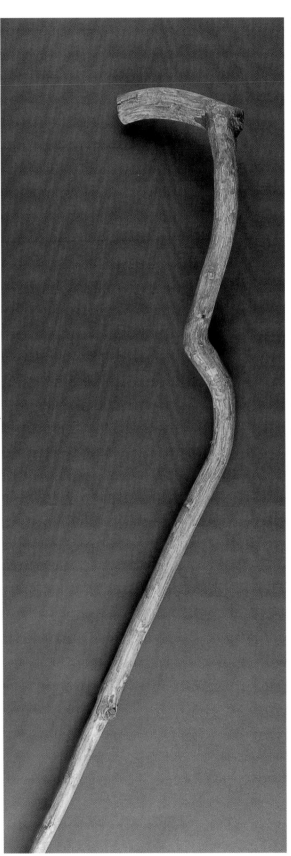

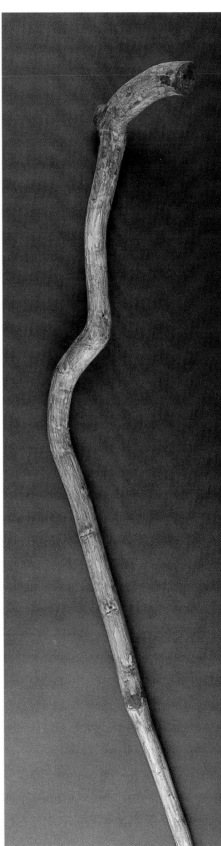